PUMPKIN CARVING STENCILS, 66 SCARY DESIGNS

V. L. HAUNTBOURNE

COVER ILLUSTRATION BY ZEE QUE

INSTRUCTIONS

- Wipe the pumpkin, removing any dirt, or dust. You can use a dump cloth. Dry it with a paper towel.

- Cut the top of the pumpkin. Use a spoon to remove the seeds and any fleshy parts, leaving a 2-3 inches border depending on the size of the pumpkin.

- Choose the desired pattern from the book.

- Cut the page out using scissors. Cut out the edges.

- Stick the template to the pumpkin with tape. Use a pencil or a sharp marker to mark spaced holes along the stencil lines, piercing the paper.

- Cut out any previously traced lines using a special pumpkin carving blade or a knife.

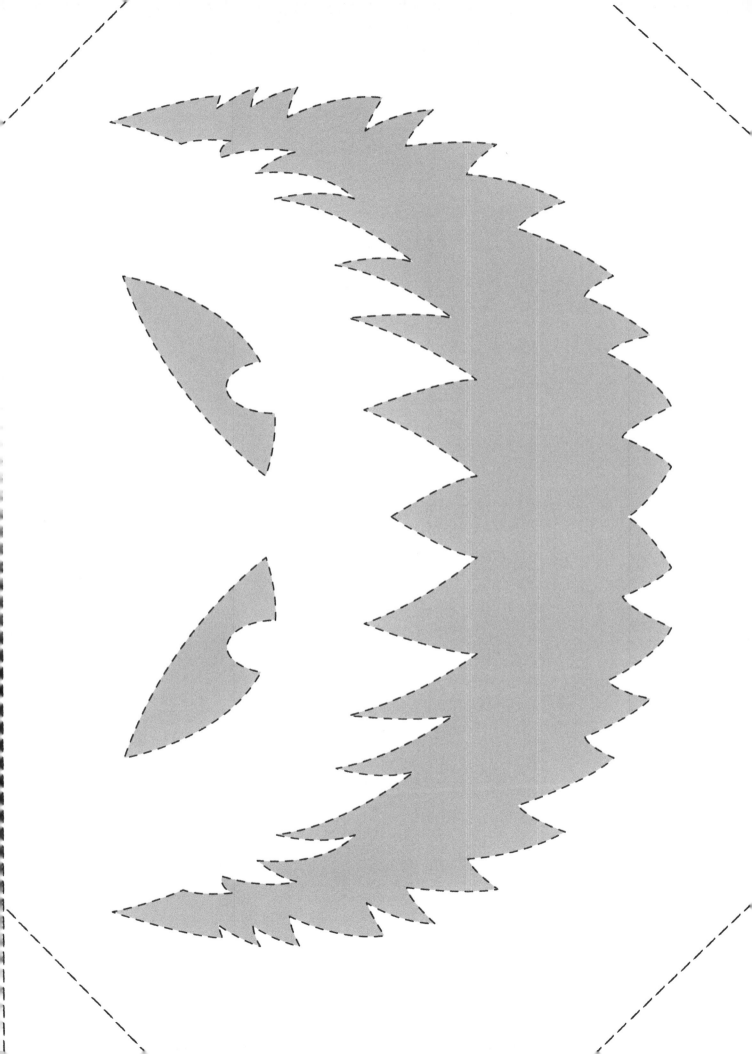

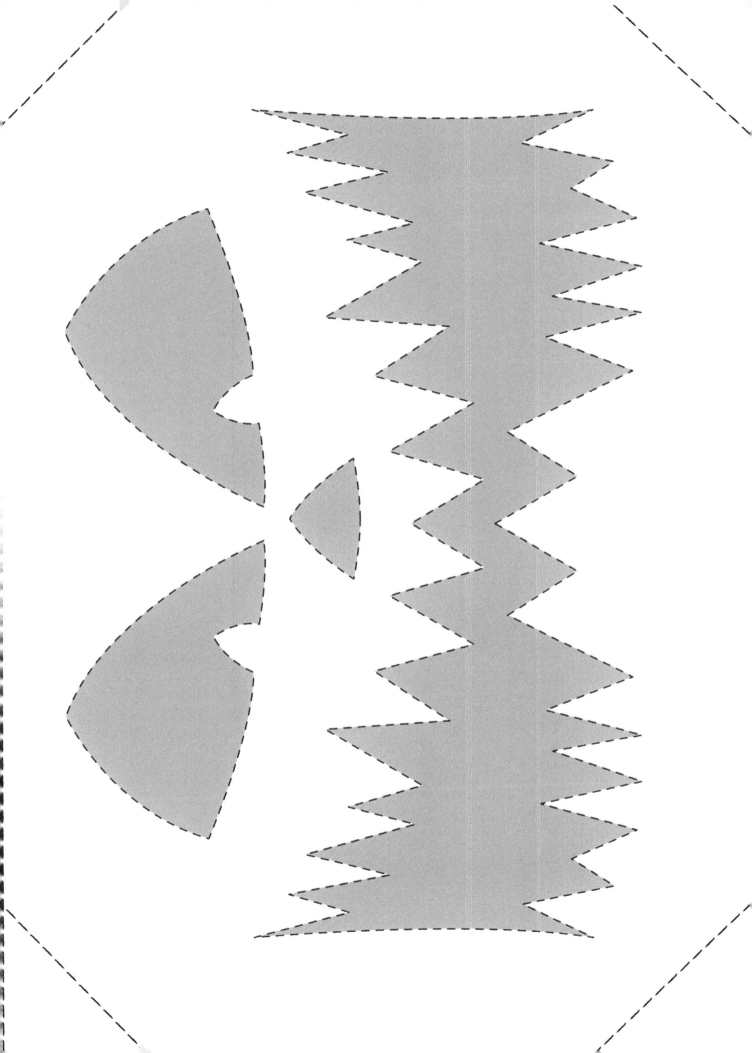

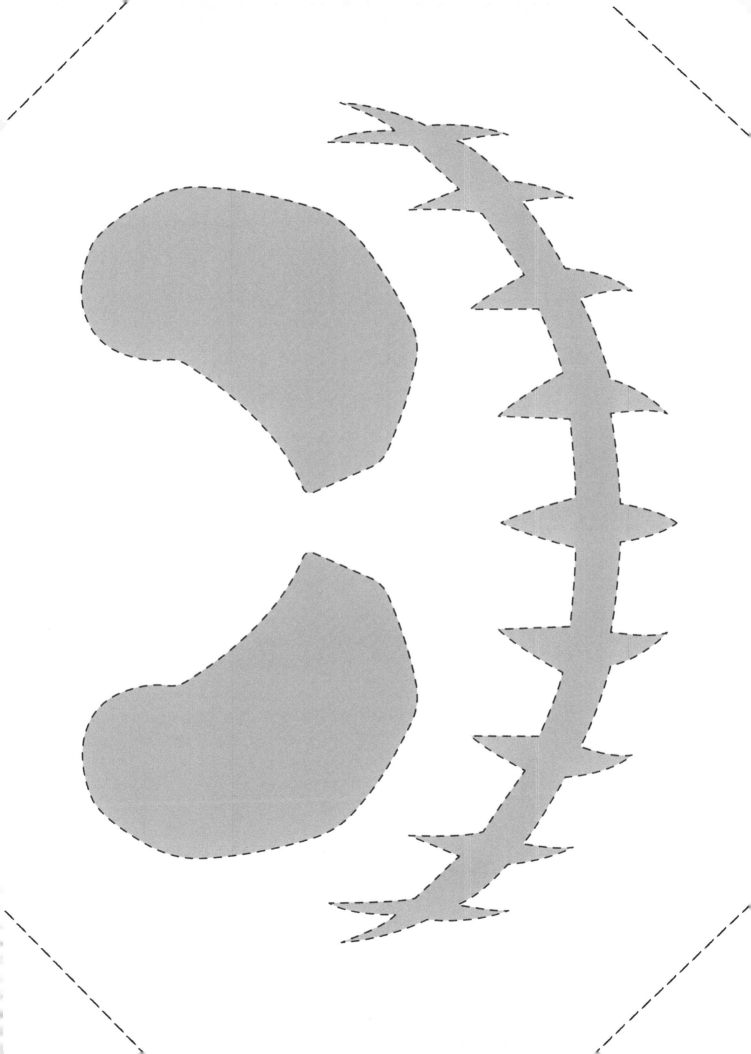

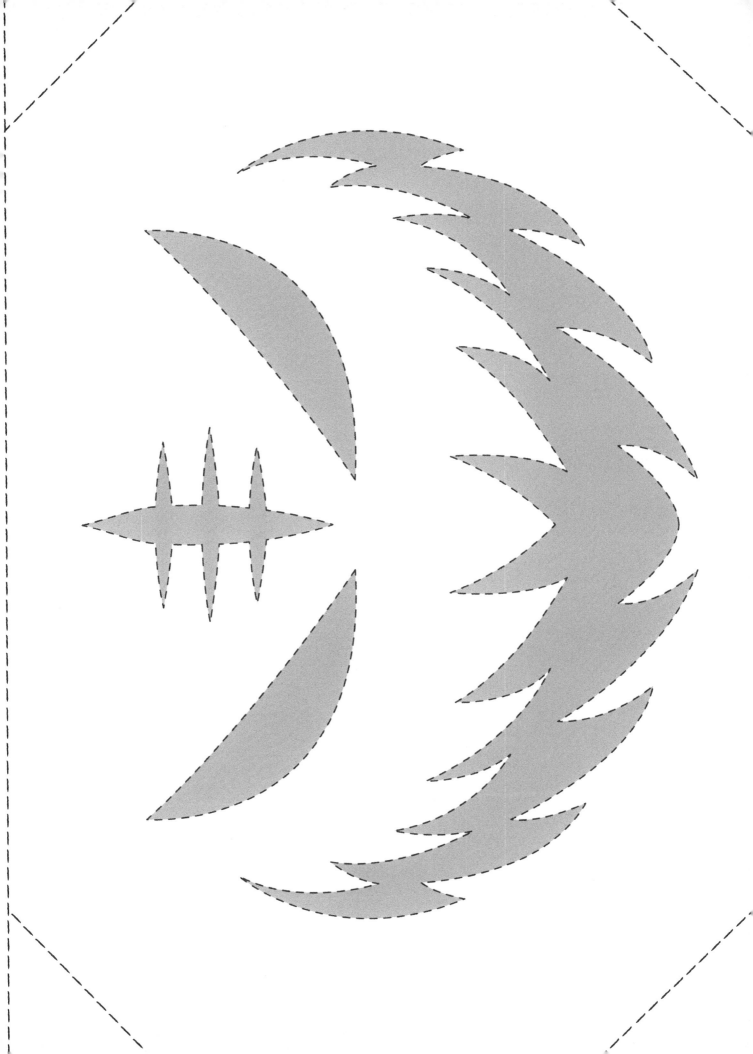

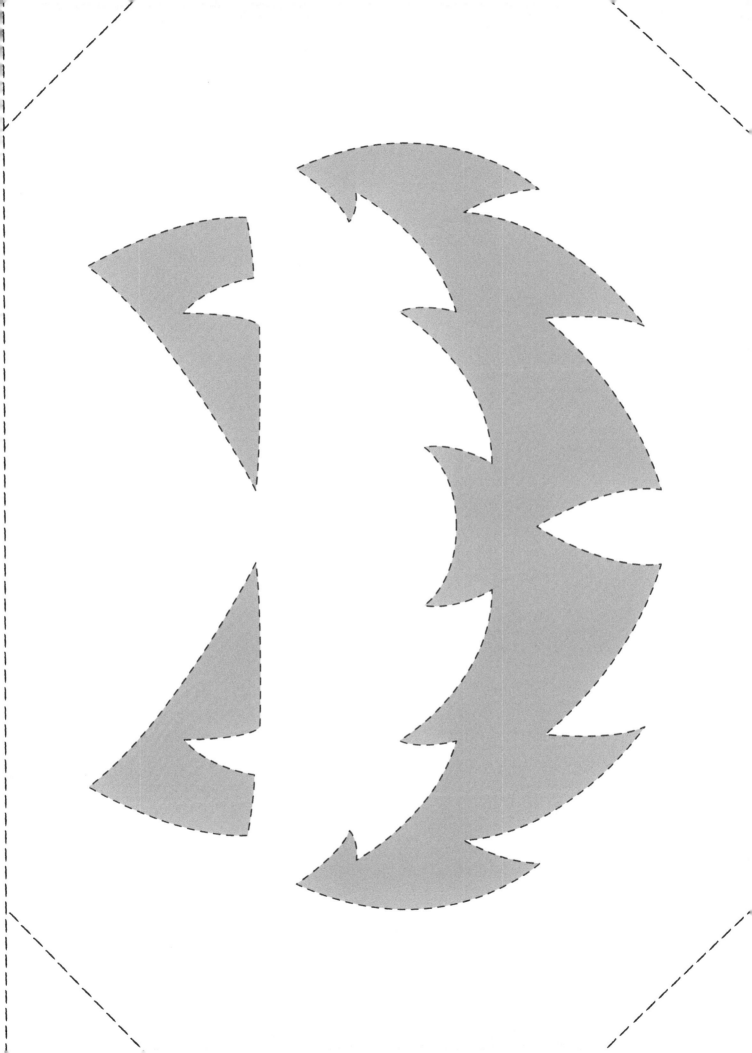

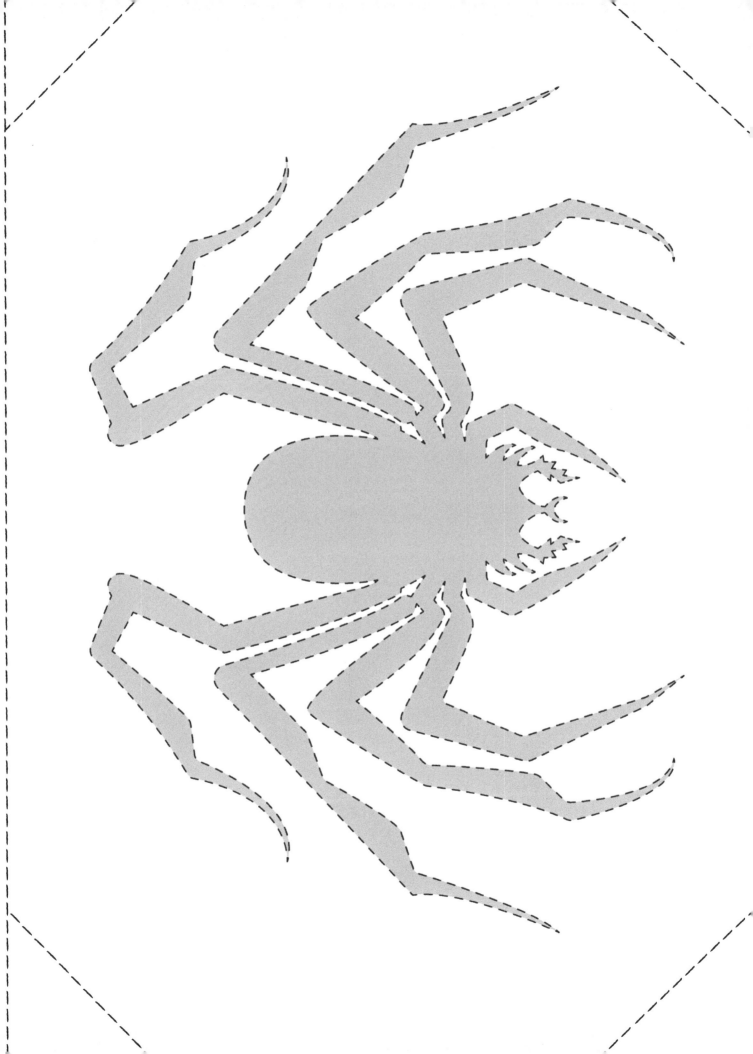

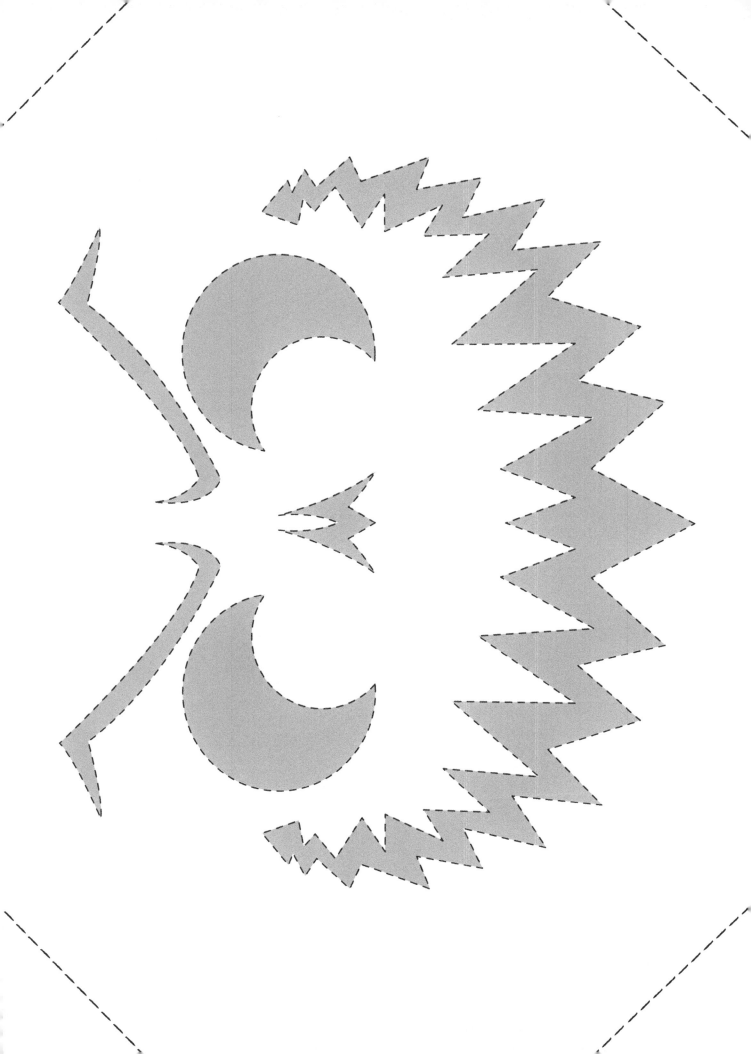

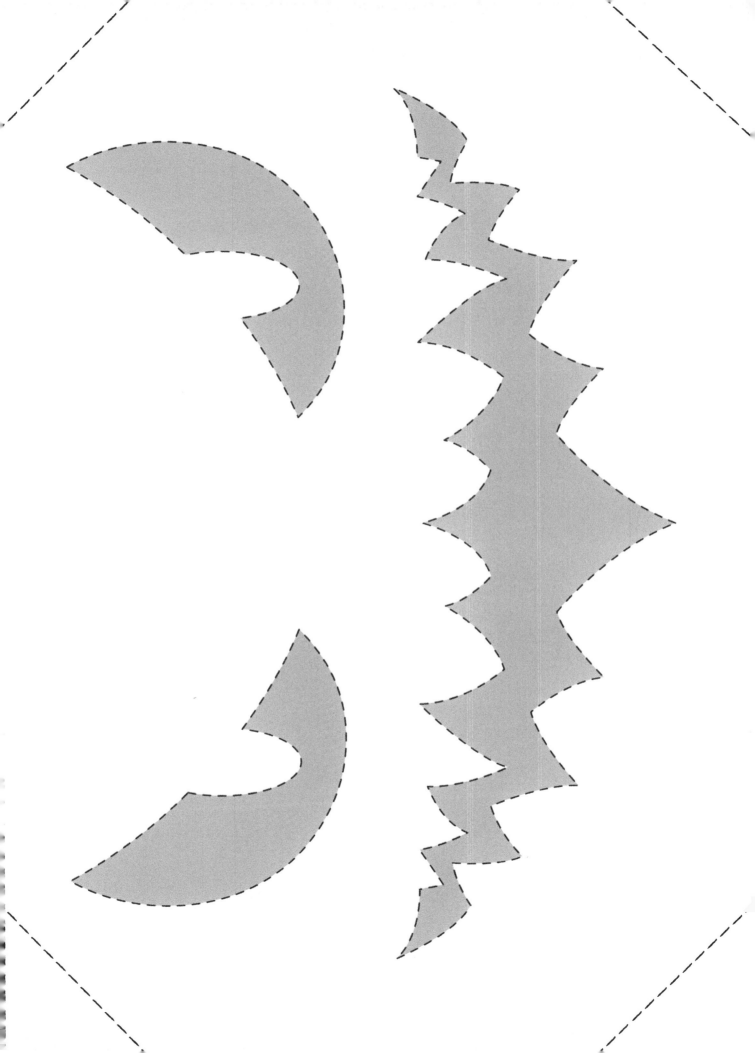

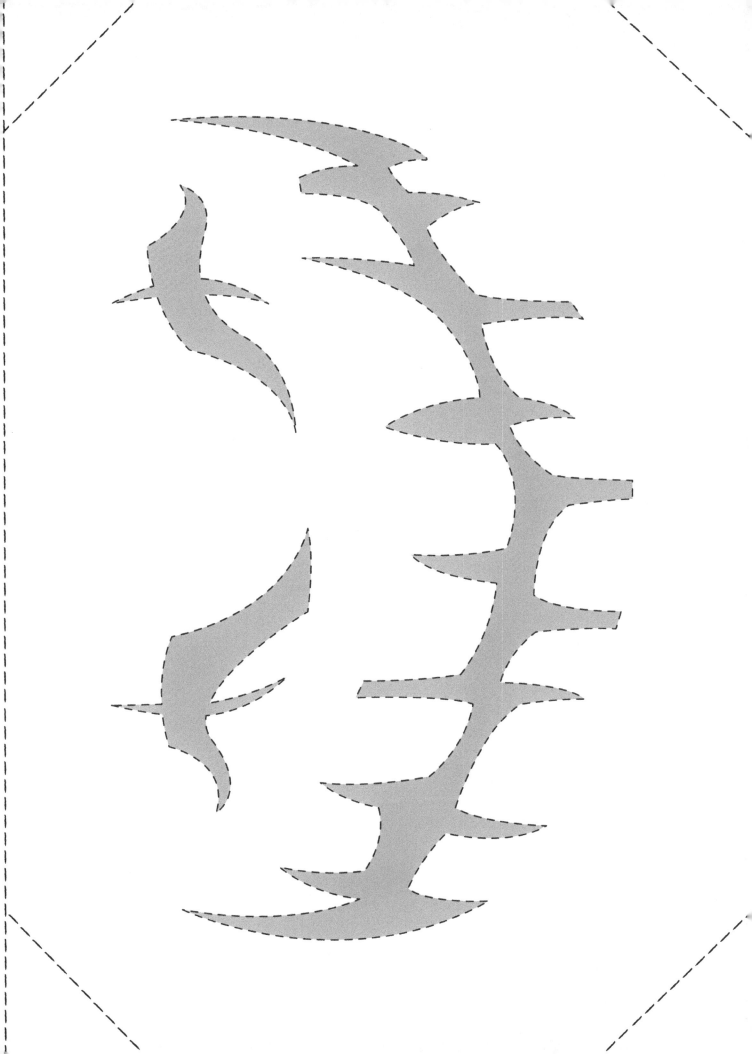

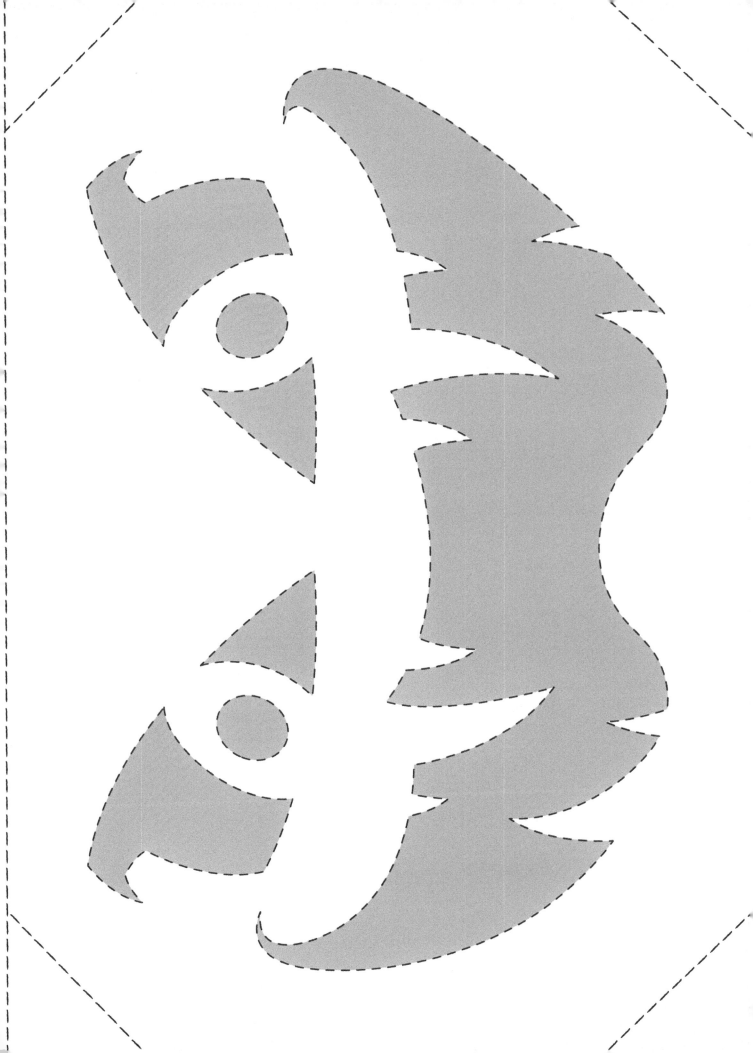

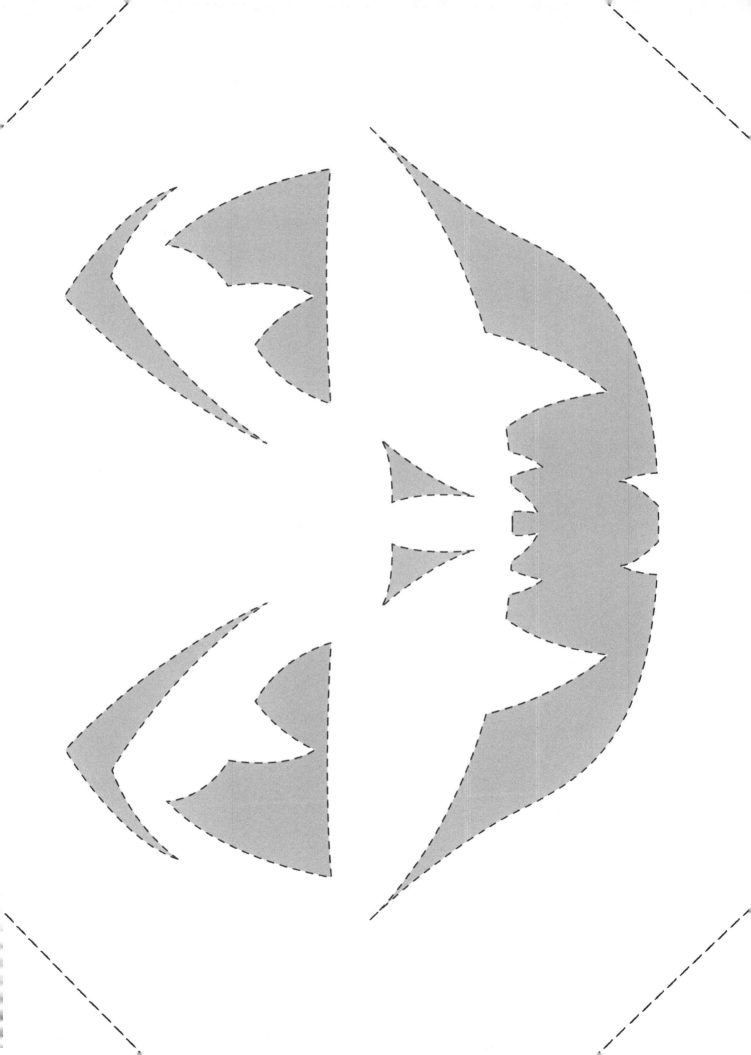

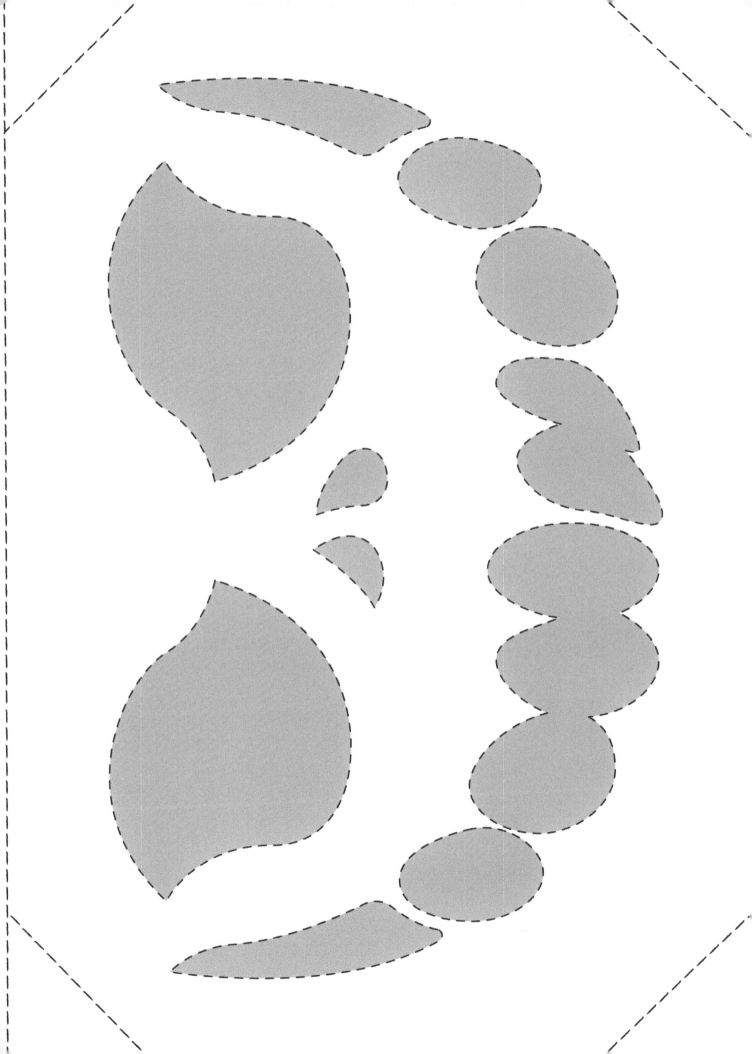

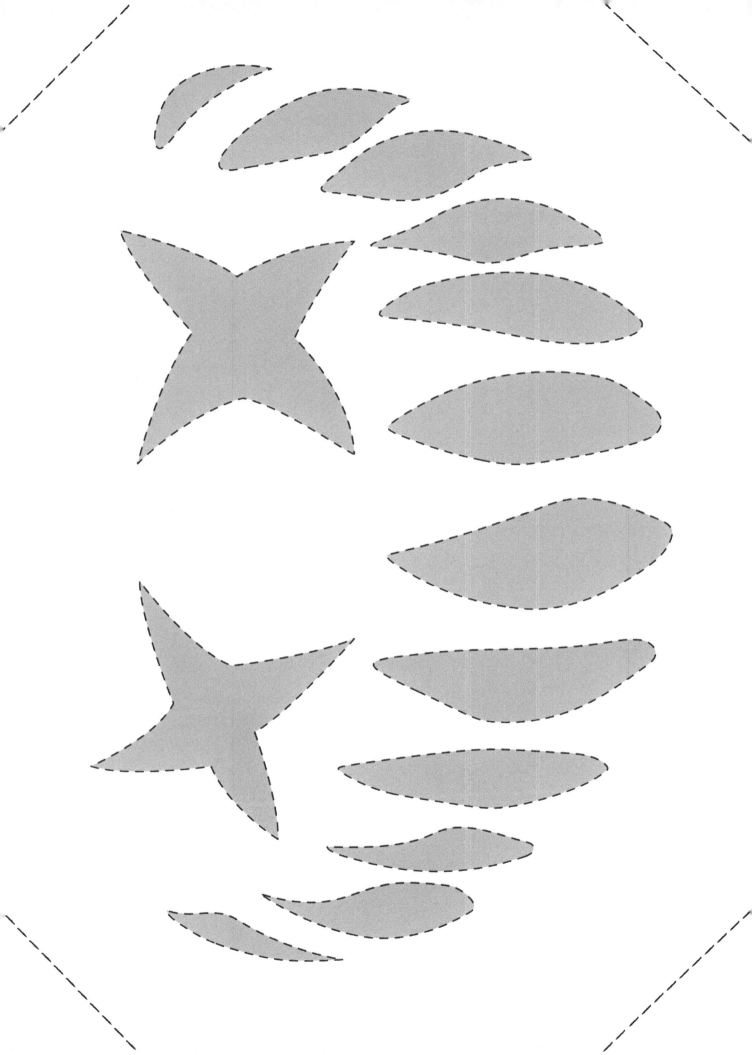

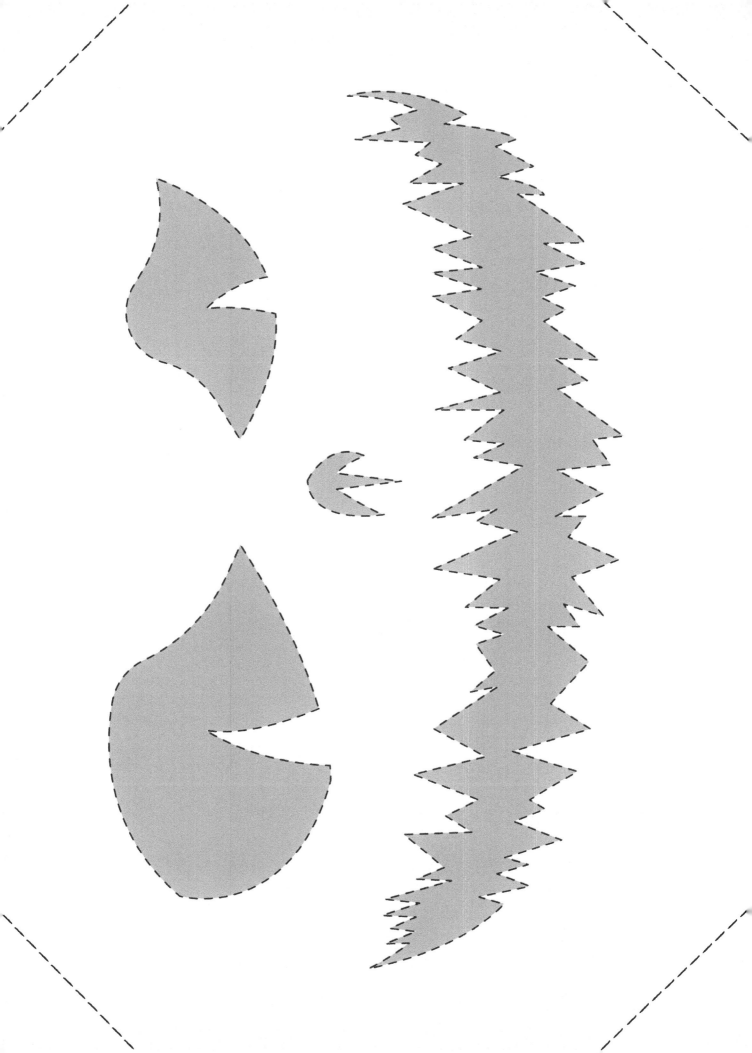

Made in the USA
Las Vegas, NV
21 October 2023

79489622R00077